PROMISES, PROMISES

2   A Fact Can Be a Beautiful Thing

8   Half as Big as Life

18   A House Is Not a Home

13   I Say a Little Prayer

22   I'll Never Fall in Love Again

30   Knowing When to Leave

36   Promises, Promises

40   She Likes Basketball

27   Upstairs

46   Wanting Things

49   Whoever You Are, I Love You

52   You'll Think of Someone

ISBN 978-1-4234-9639-7

HAL•LEONARD®
CORPORATION
7777 W. BLUEMOUND RD. P.O. BOX 13819 MILWAUKEE, WI 53213

Visit Hal Leonard Online at
www.halleonard.com

A FACT CAN BE A BEAUTIFUL THING

Lyric by HAL DAVID
Music by BURT BACHARACH

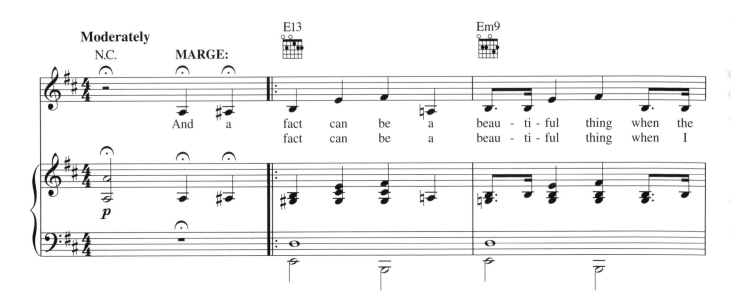

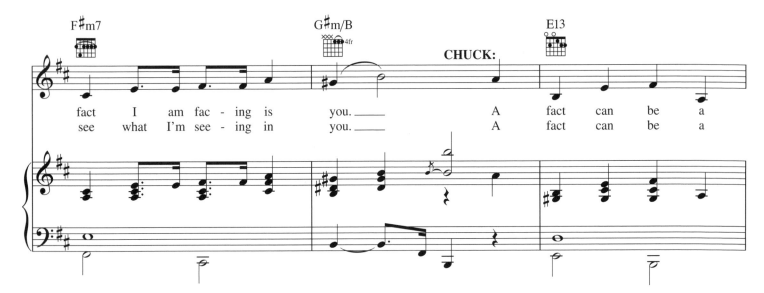

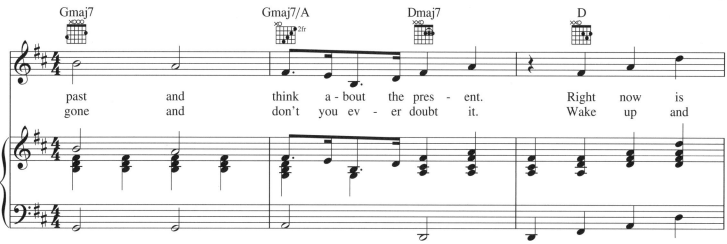

past and think about the pres - ent. Right now is
gone and don't you ev - er doubt it. Wake up is and

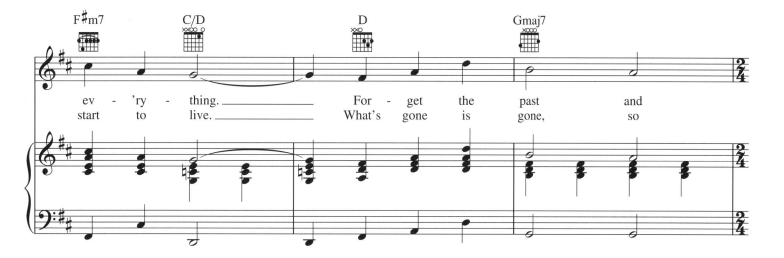

ev - 'ry - thing. _____ For - get the past and
start to live. _____ What's gone is gone, so

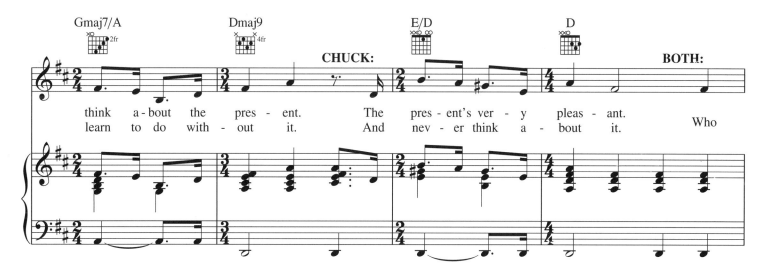

CHUCK:
BOTH:

think a - bout the pres - ent. The pres - ent's ver - y pleas - ant.
learn to do with - out it. And nev - er think a - bout it.
Who

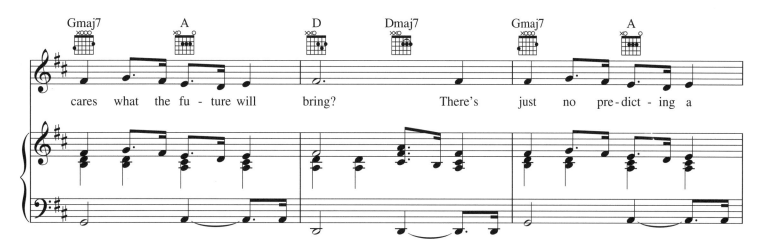

cares what the fu - ture will bring? There's just no pre - dict - ing a

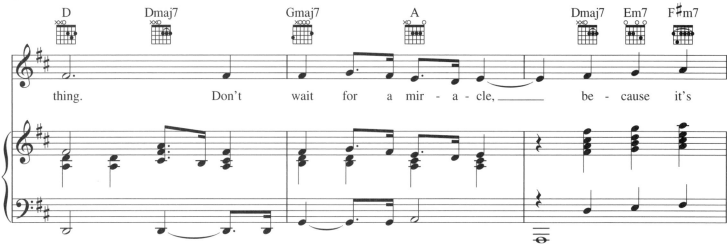

thing. Don't wait for a mir - a - cle, _____ be - cause it's

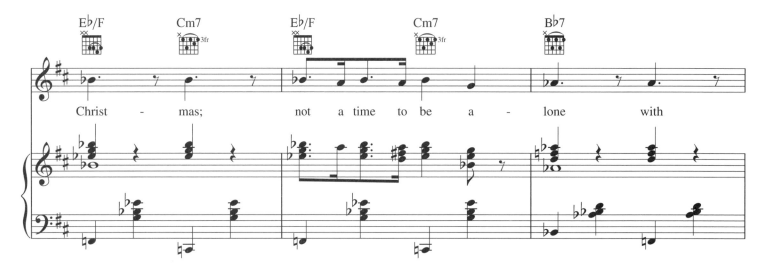

Christ - mas; not a time to be a - lone with

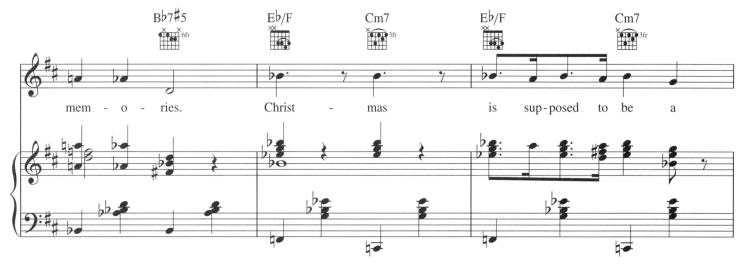

mem - o - ries. Christ - mas is sup - posed to be a

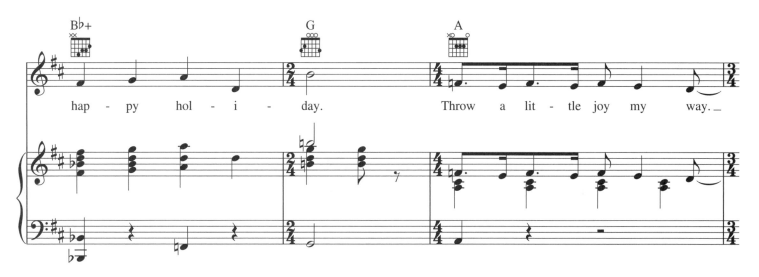

hap - py hol - i - day. Throw a lit - tle joy my way. _____

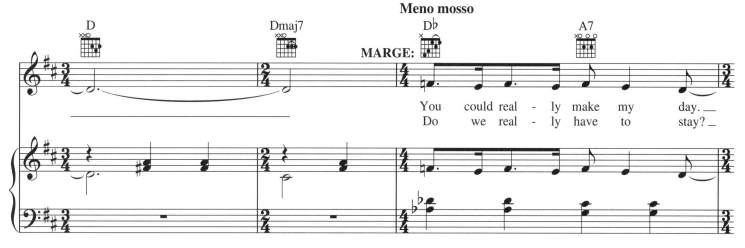

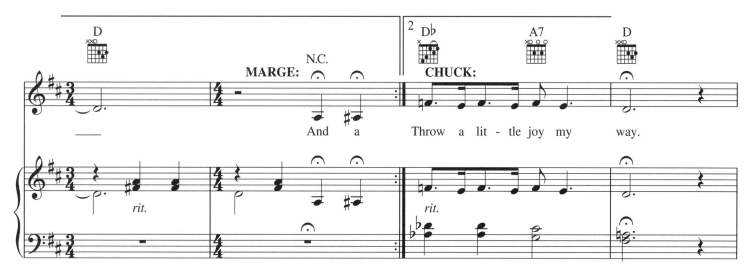

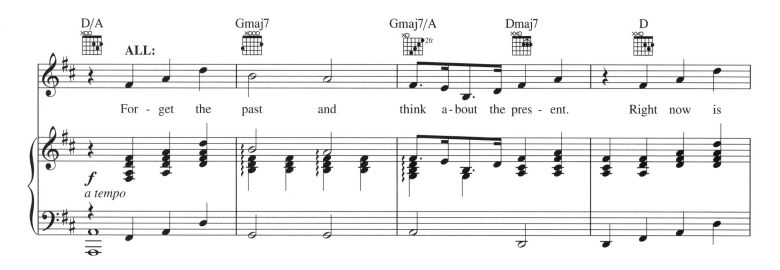

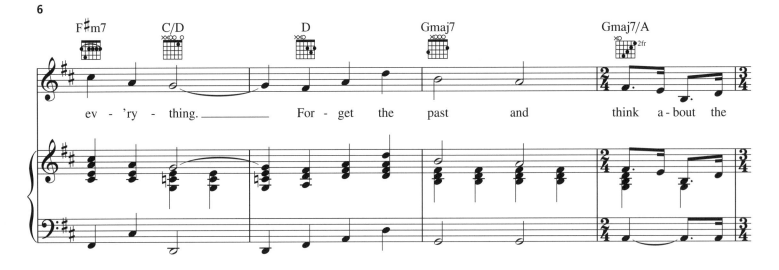

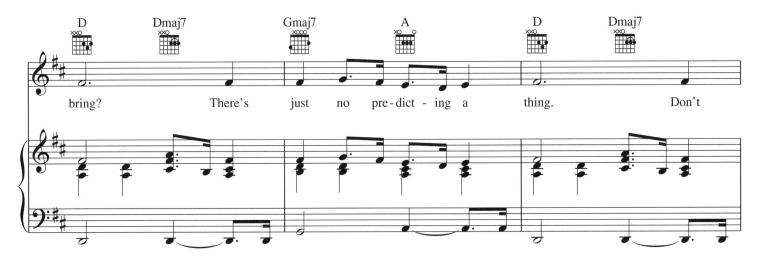

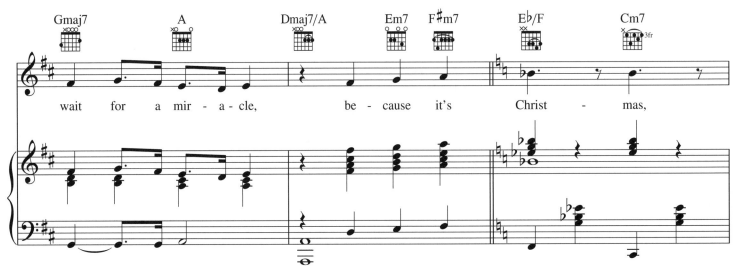

just the per-fect night for us to dance and sing. Christ-mas

is sup-posed to be a hap-py hol-i - day,

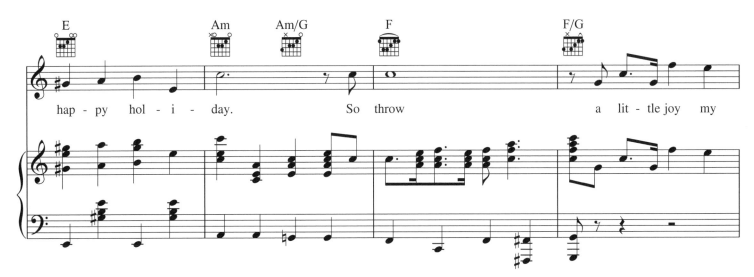

hap-py hol-i - day. So throw a lit-tle joy my

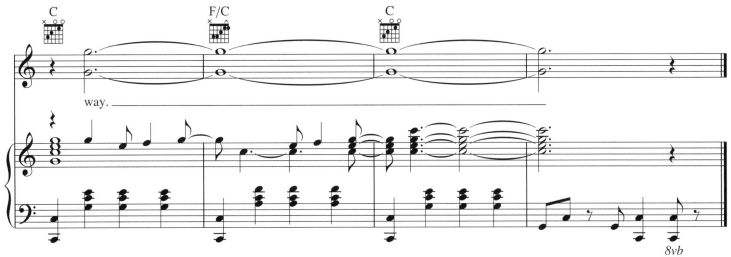

way. _____

8vb

HALF AS BIG AS LIFE

Lyric by HAL DAVID
Music by BURT BACHARACH

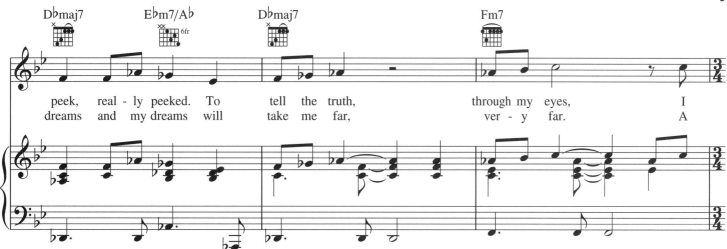

peek, real - ly peeked. To tell the truth, through my eyes, I A
dreams and my dreams will take me far, ver - y far. A

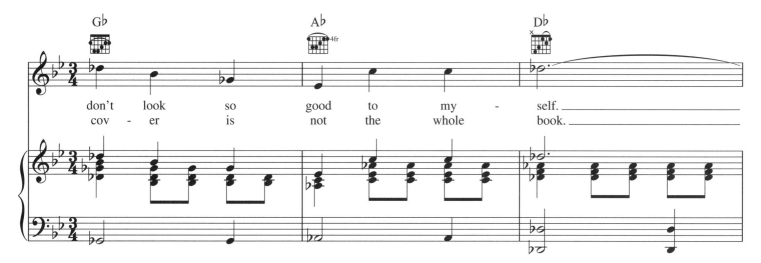

don't look so good to my - self. _____
cov - er is not the whole book. _____

___ Half as big as
___ Half as big as

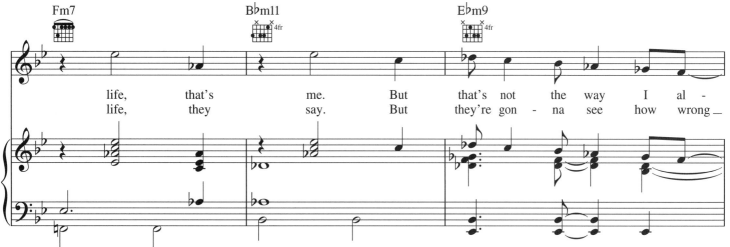

life, that's me. But that's not the way I al -
life, they say. But they're gon - na see how wrong ___

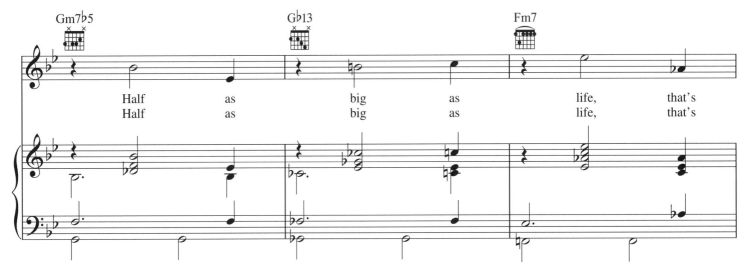

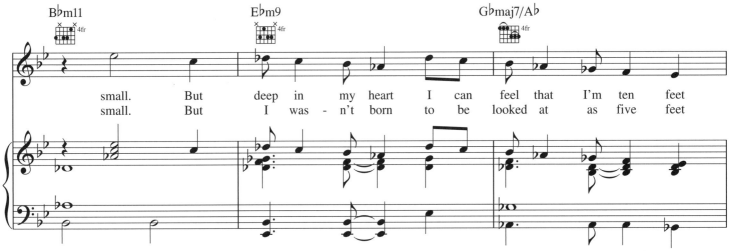

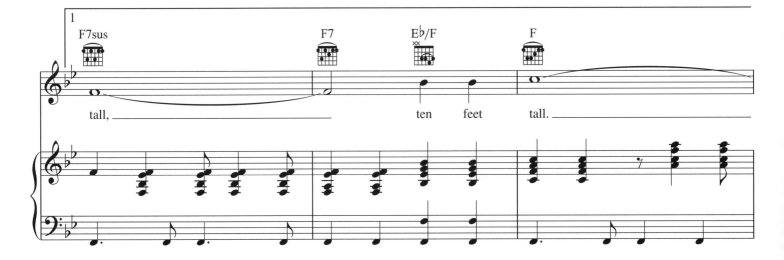

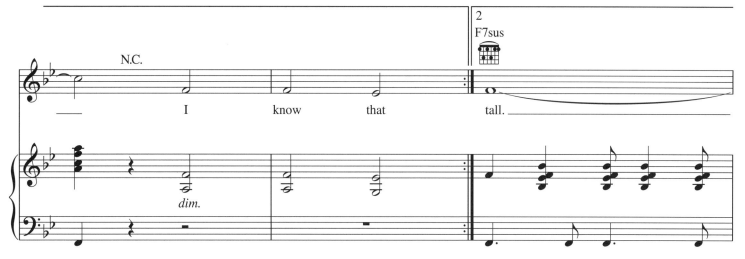

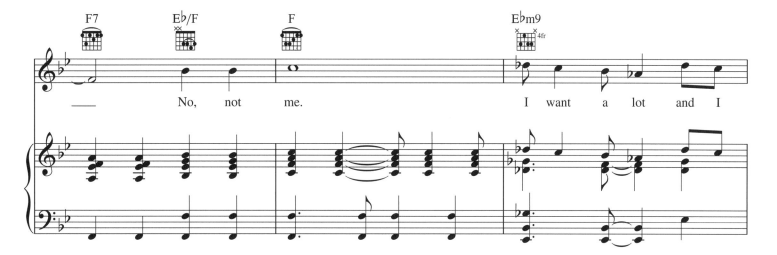

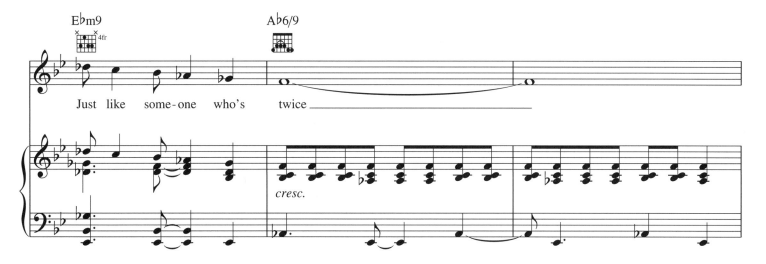

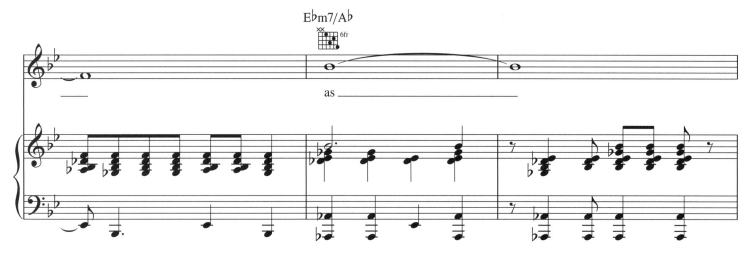

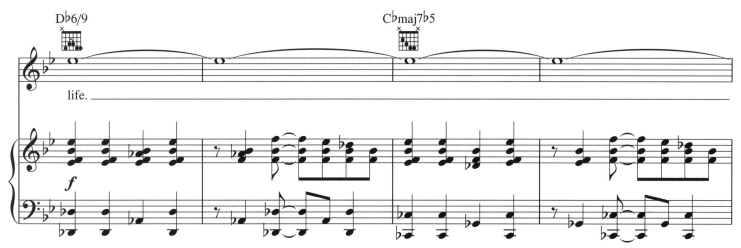

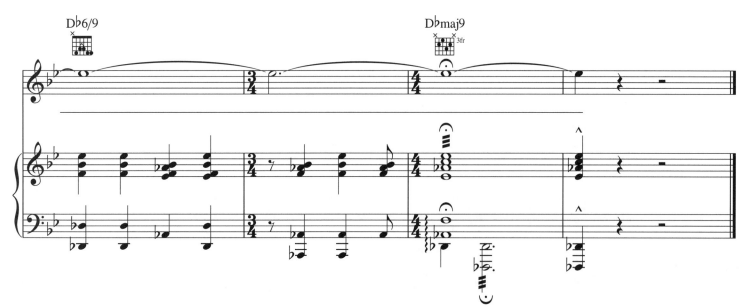

I SAY A LITTLE PRAYER

Lyric by HAL DAVID
Music by BURT BACHARACH

Moderately fast

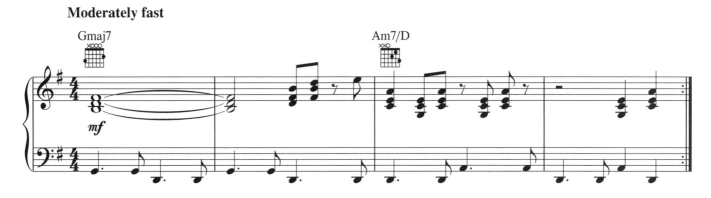

FRAN:

The mo - ment I
I run ___ for the

Instrumental solo

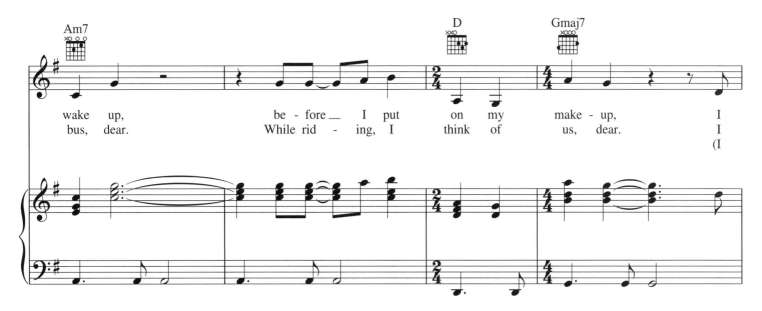

wake up,   be - fore ___ I put   on my   make - up,   I
bus, dear.   While rid - ing, I   think of   us, dear.   I I
                                                                                              (I

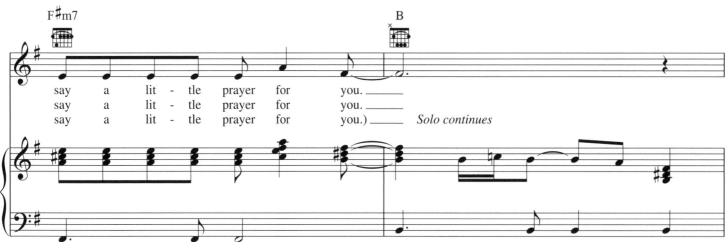

say a lit - tle prayer for you. _____
say a lit - tle prayer for you. _____
say a lit - tle prayer for you.) _____ *Solo continues*

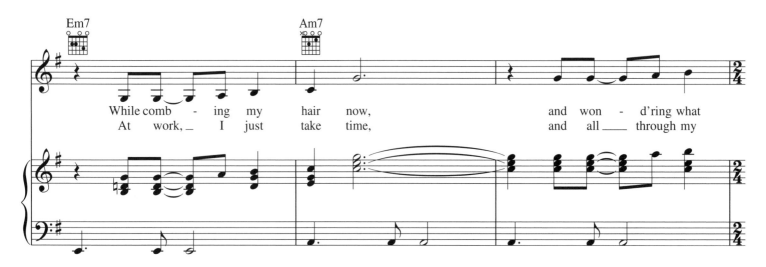

While comb - ing my hair now, and won - d'ring what
At work, _ I just hair take time, and all _ through my

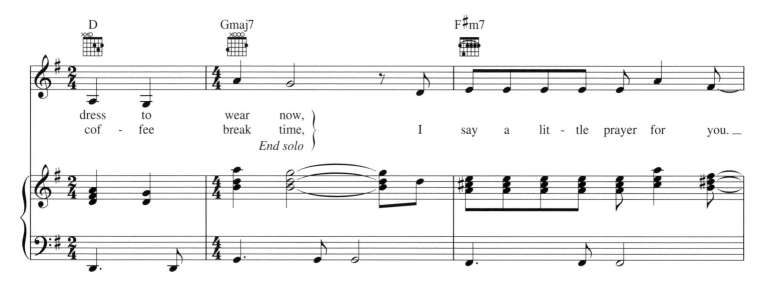

dress to wear now,
cof - fee break time, *End solo*
I say a lit - tle prayer for you. _

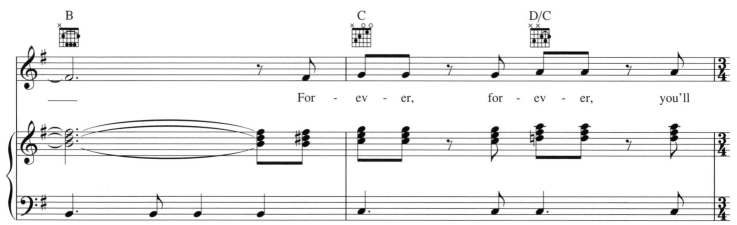

_____ For - ev - er, for - ev - er, you'll

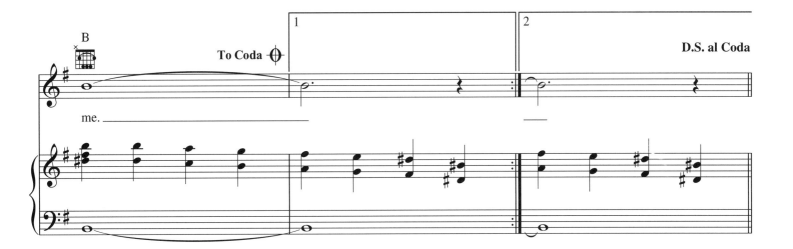

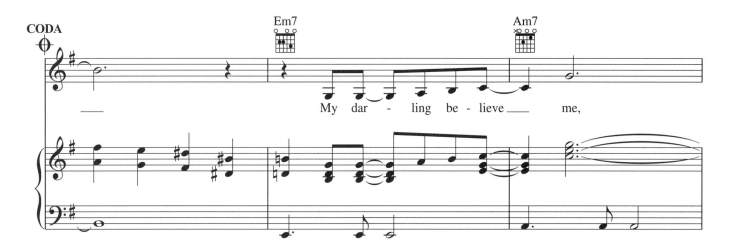

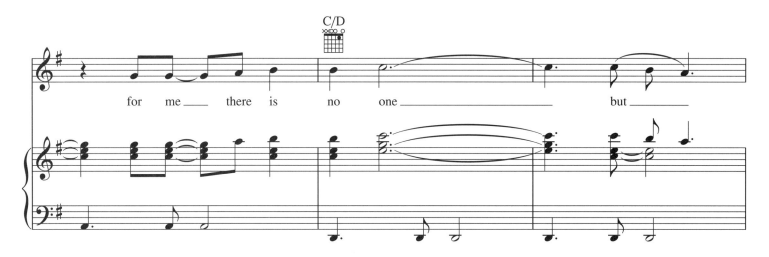

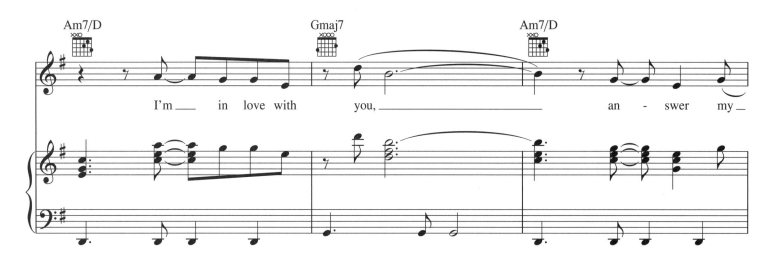

prayer. Say __ you love me, too. __

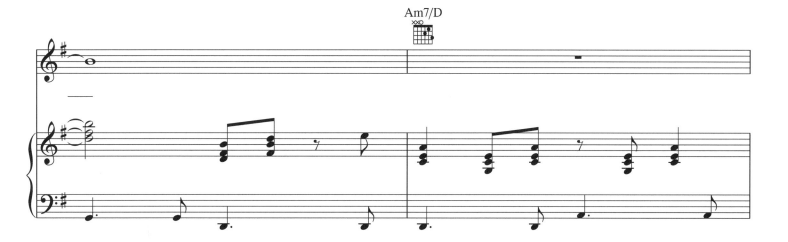

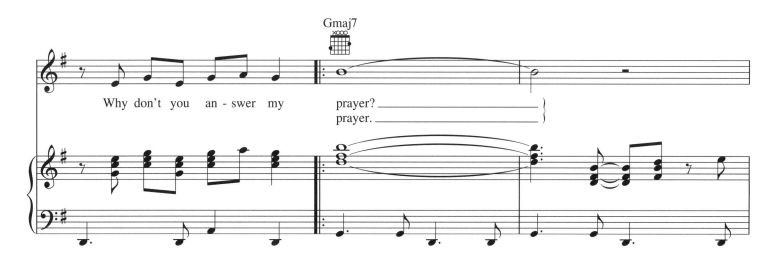

Why don't you an-swer my prayer? __
prayer. __

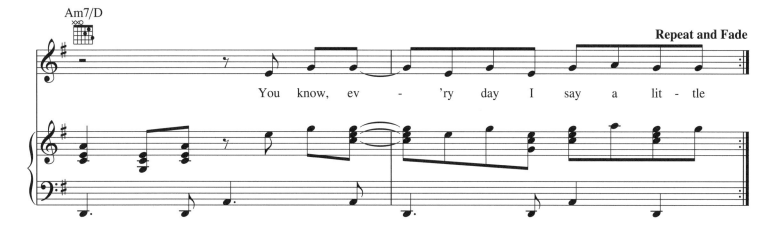

Repeat and Fade

You know, ev-'ry day I say a lit-tle

A HOUSE IS NOT A HOME

Lyric by HAL DAVID
Music by BURT BACHARACH

Slowly and expressively

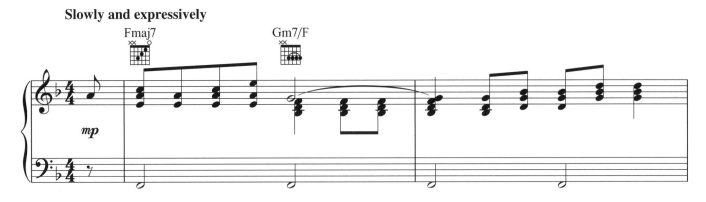

FRAN:

A chair is still a chair ____

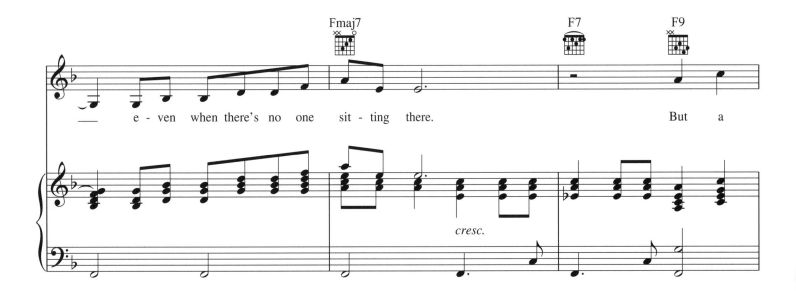

____ e - ven when there's no one sit - ting there. But a

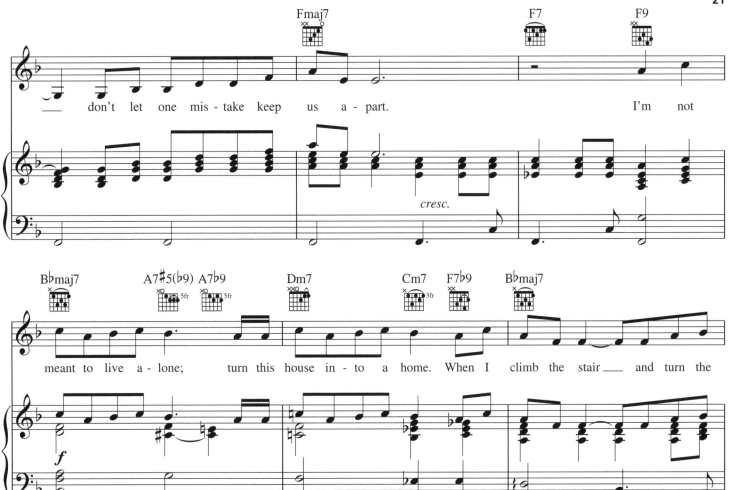

Fmaj7 · F7 · F9

don't let one mis-take keep us a-part. I'm not

cresc.

Bbmaj7 · A7#5(b9) A7b9 · Dm7 · Cm7 F7b9 · Bbmaj7

meant to live a-lone; turn this house in-to a home. When I climb the stair____ and turn the

f

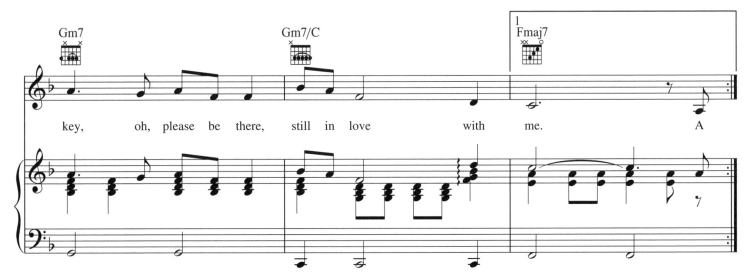

Gm7 · Gm7/C · 1. Fmaj7

key, oh, please be there, still in love with me. A

2. Fmaj7

me.____

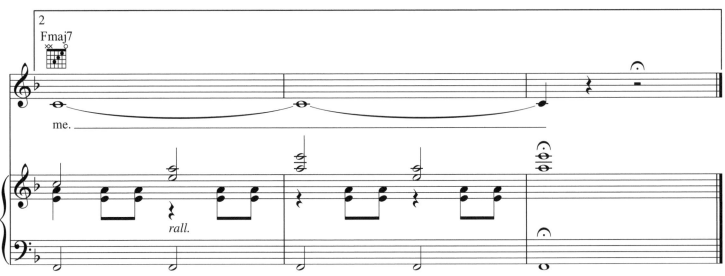

rall.

I'LL NEVER FALL IN LOVE AGAIN

Lyric by HAL DAVID
Music by BURT BACHARACH

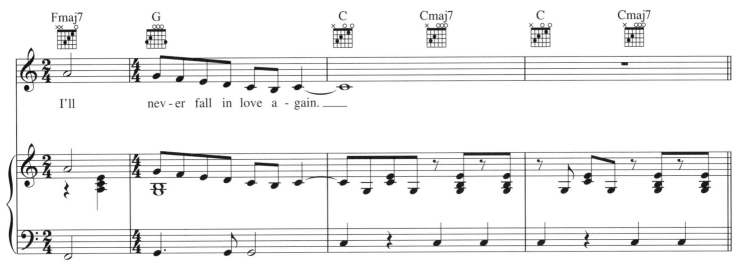

I'll nev-er fall in love a-gain. _____

What do you get when you kiss a guy? _ You get e-nough germs to catch _

CHUCK: What do you get when you give your heart? You get it all bro-ken up _

_____ pneu-mo - nia. Af - ter you do, he'll nev - er phone _ ya.

_____ and bat - tered. That's what you get, a heart that's shat - tered.

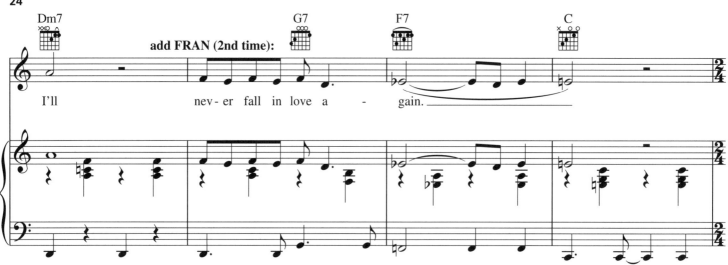

I'll nev-er fall in love a - gain.

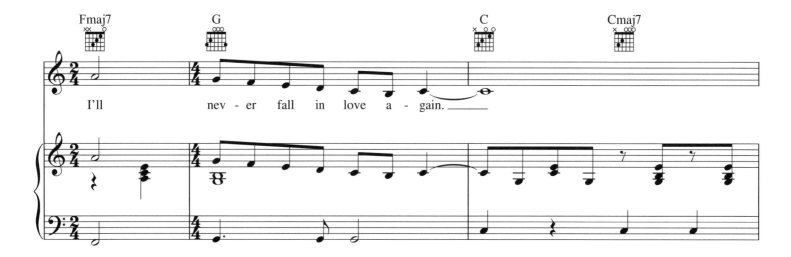

I'll nev-er fall in love a - gain.

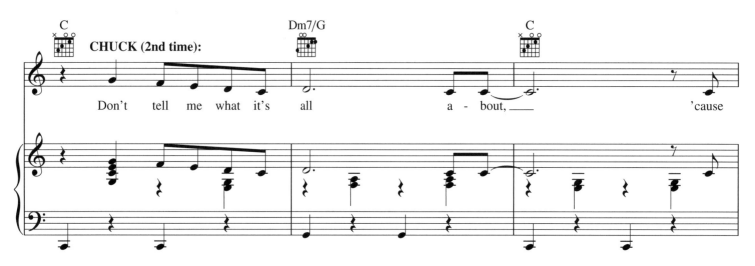

CHUCK (2nd time):

Don't tell me what it's all a - bout, _____ 'cause

I've been there _ and I'm glad I'm out. _____ Out of those chains, those

FRAN (2nd time):
chains that bind ___ you. That is why I'm here to re- mind you:

BOTH (2nd time):
What do you get when you fall in love? ___ You on - ly get lies and pain ___

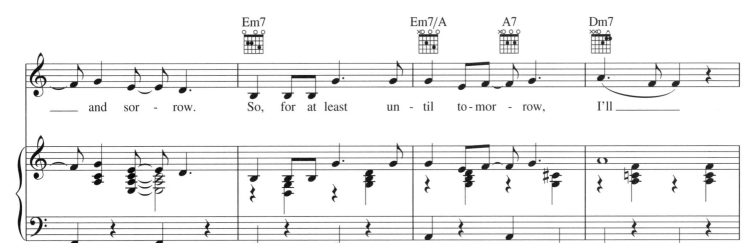

___ and sor - row. So, for at least un - til to- mor - row, I'll ___

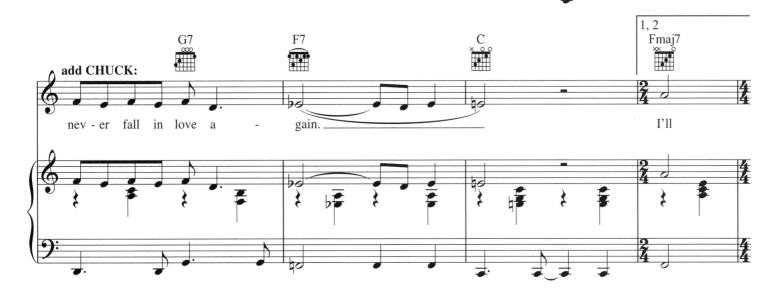

add CHUCK:
nev - er fall in love a - gain. ___ I'll

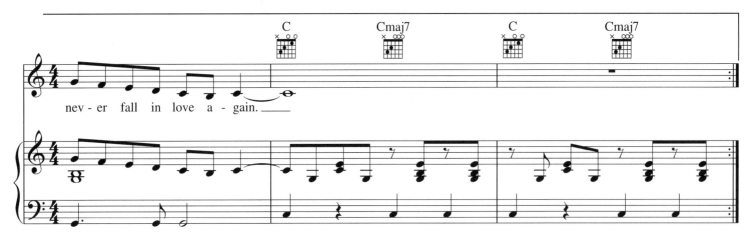

nev - er fall in love a - gain. _____

I'll   nev - er fall in love a - gain. _____

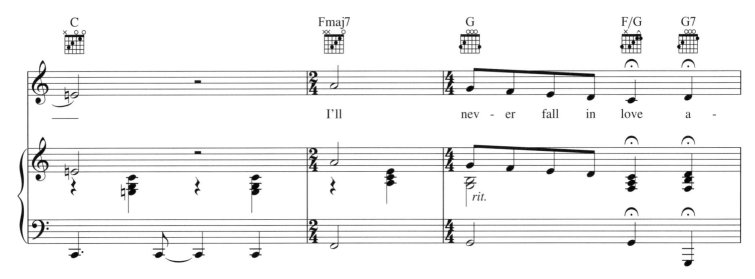

I'll   nev - er fall in love a -

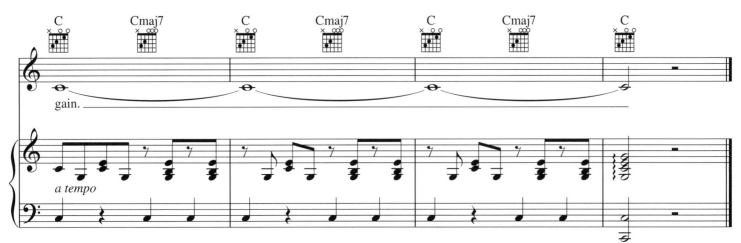

gain. _____

UPSTAIRS

Lyric by HAL DAVID
Music by BURT BACHARACH

Moderately fast

CHUCK:

Up - stairs,

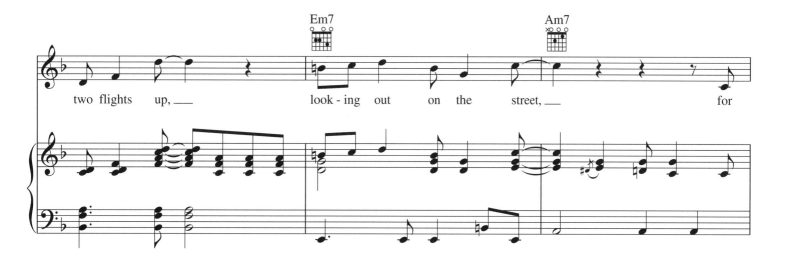

two flights up, ___ look - ing out on the street, ___ for

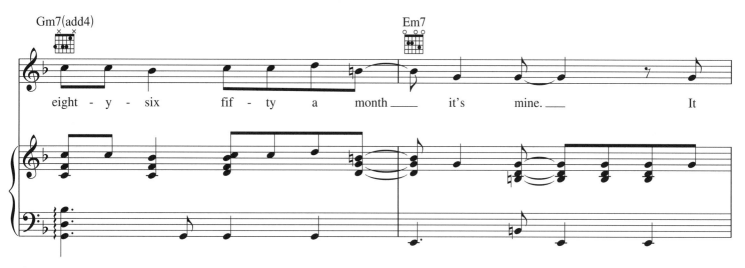

eight - y - six fif - ty a month ___ it's mine. ___ It

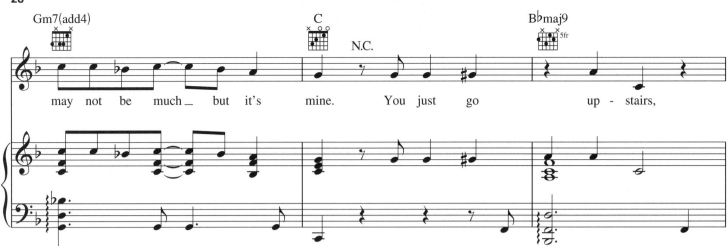

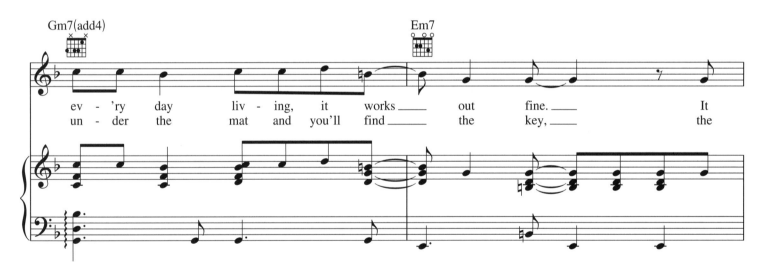

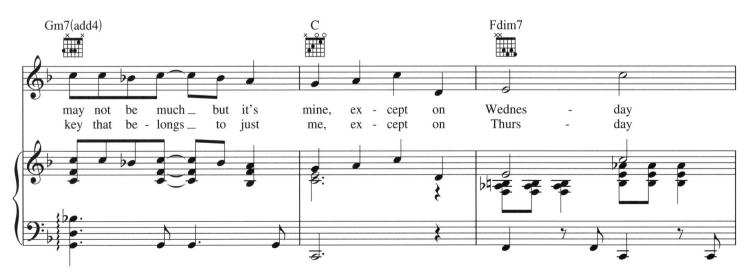

KNOWING WHEN TO LEAVE

Lyric by HAL DAVID
Music by BURT BACHARACH

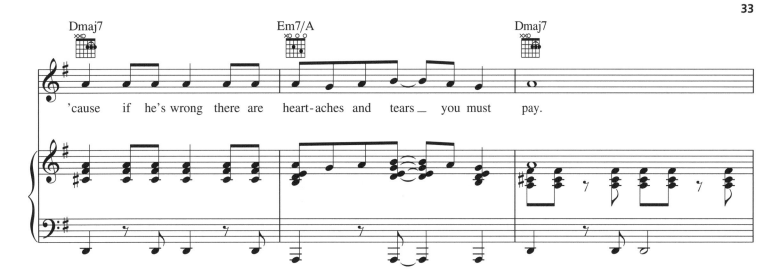

'cause if he's wrong there are heart-aches and tears— you must pay.

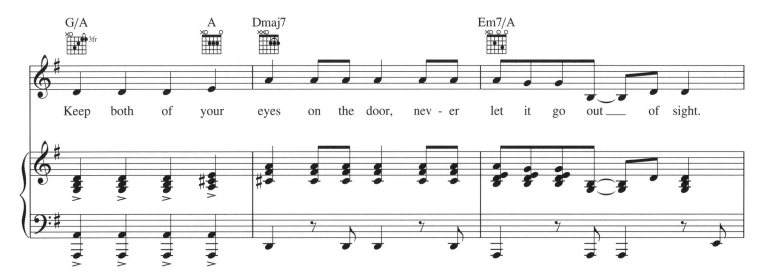

Keep both of your eyes on the door, nev-er let it go out— of sight.

Just be pre-pared when the time has come for you to run a - way.—

pp sub.

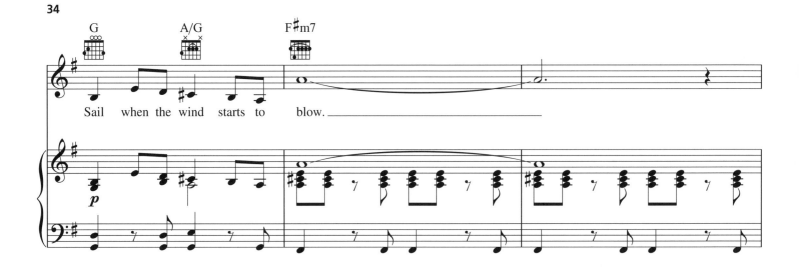

Sail when the wind starts to blow.

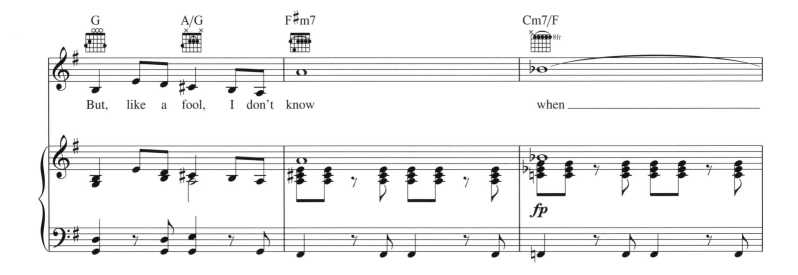

But, like a fool, I don't know when

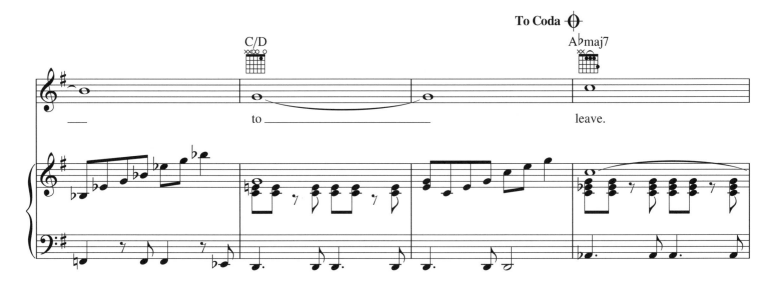

To Coda

to leave.

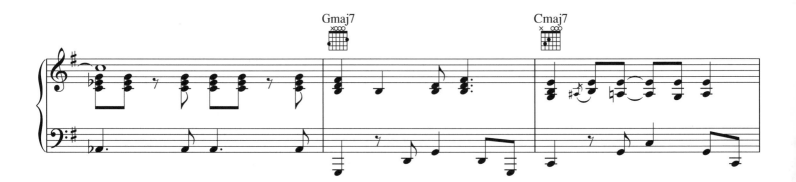

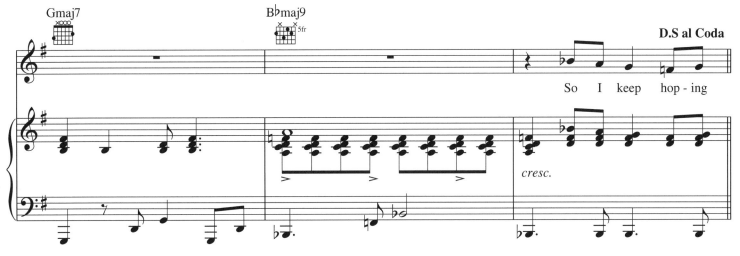

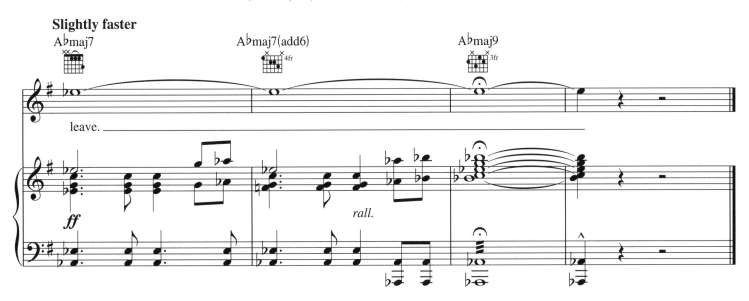

PROMISES, PROMISES

Lyric by HAL DAVID
Music by BURT BACHARACH

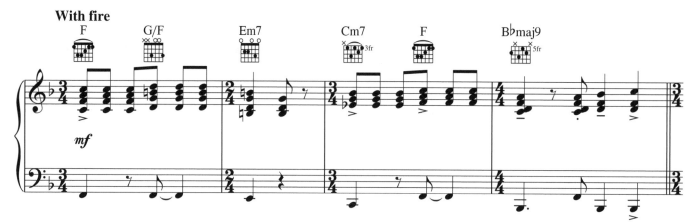

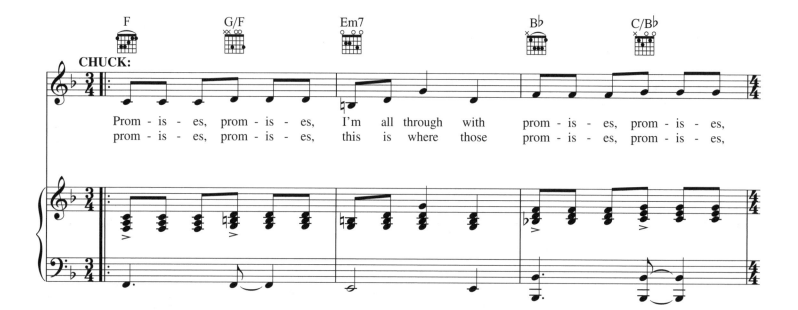

Prom - is - es, prom - is - es, I'm all through with prom - is - es, prom - is - es,
prom - is - es, prom - is - es, this is where those prom - is - es, prom - is - es,

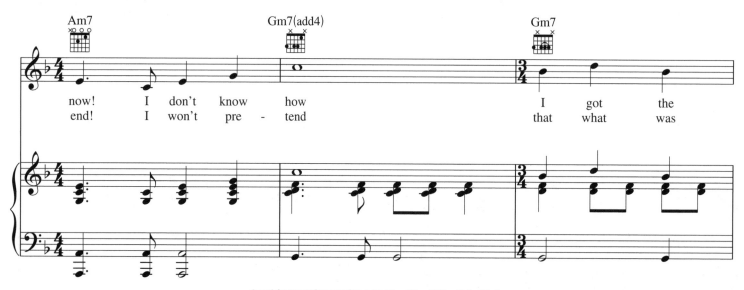

now! I don't know how
end! I won't pre - tend

I got the
that what was

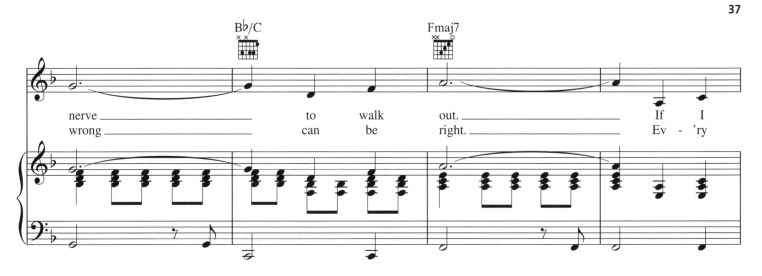

nerve _____ to walk out. _____ If I
wrong _____ can be right. _____ Ev - 'ry

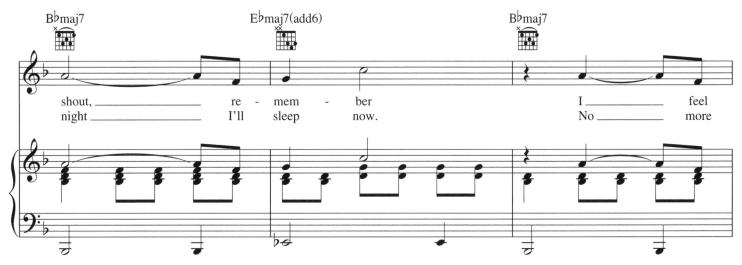

shout, _____ re - mem - ber I _____ feel
night _____ I'll sleep now. No _____ more

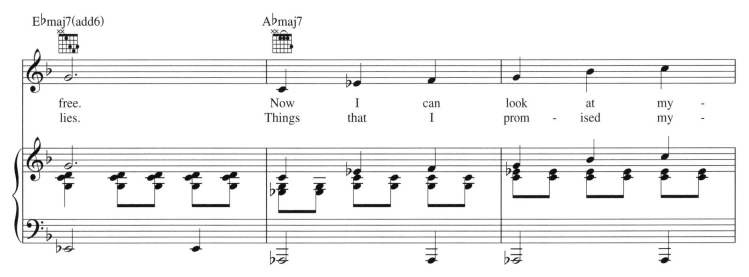

free. Now I can look at my -
lies. Things that I prom - ised my -

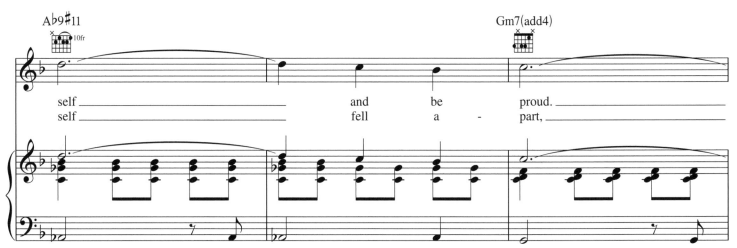

self _____ and be proud. _____
self _____ fell a - part, _____

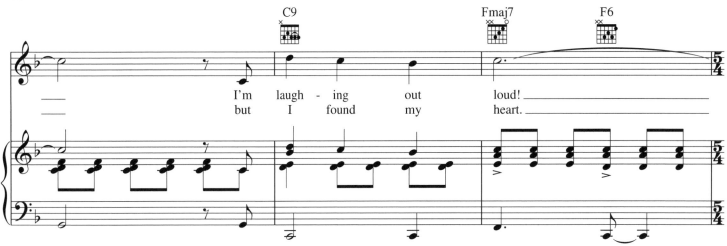

I'm laugh - ing out loud!
but I found out my heart.

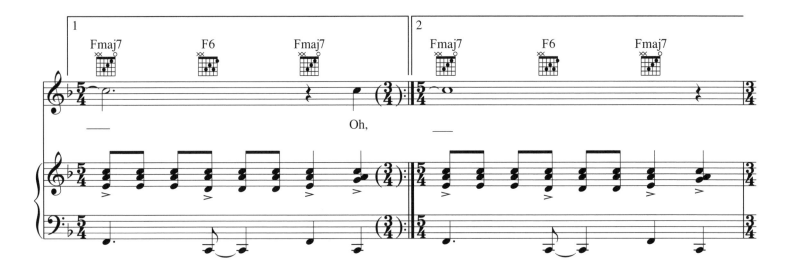

Oh,

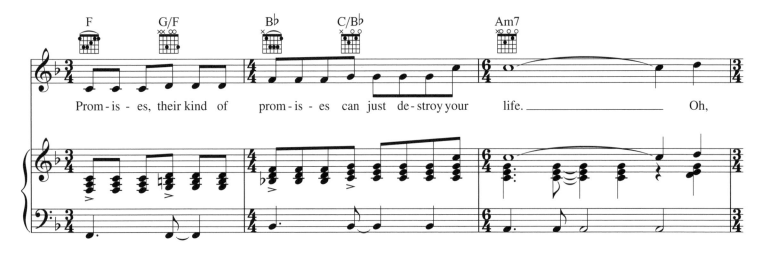

Prom - is - es, their kind of prom - is - es can just de - stroy your life. _____ Oh,

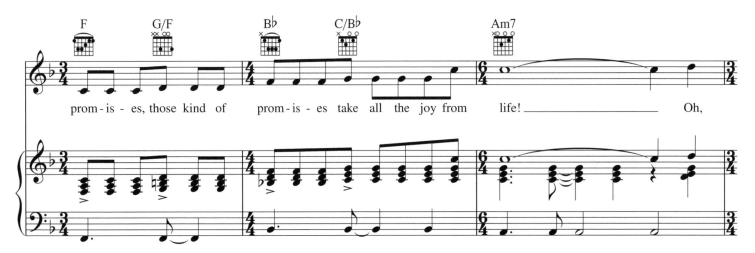

prom - is - es, those kind of prom - is - es take all the joy from life! _____ Oh,

prom-is-es, prom-is-es, my kind of prom-is-es _____ can lead to

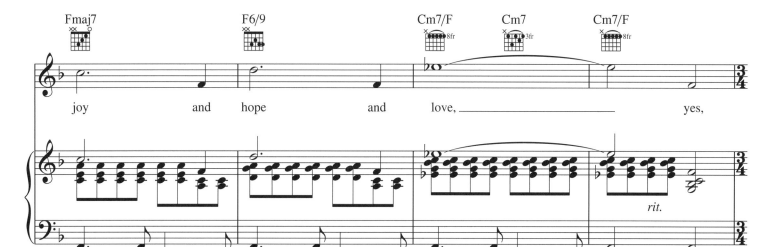

joy and hope and love, _____ yes,

love. _____

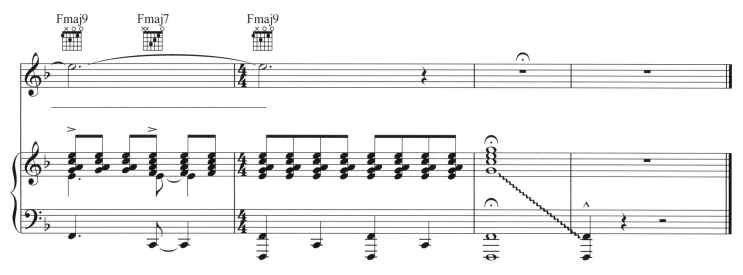

SHE LIKES BASKETBALL

Lyric by HAL DAVID
Music by BURT BACHARACH

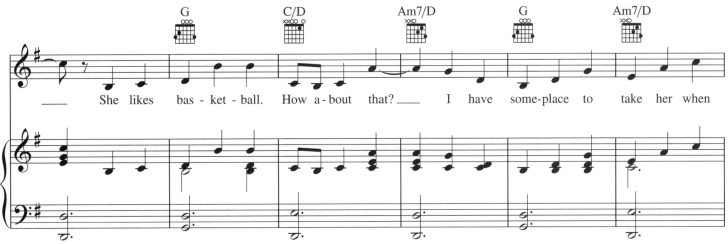

She likes bas - ket - ball. How a - bout that? ___ I have some-place to take her when

we go out. Bas - ket - ball! ___

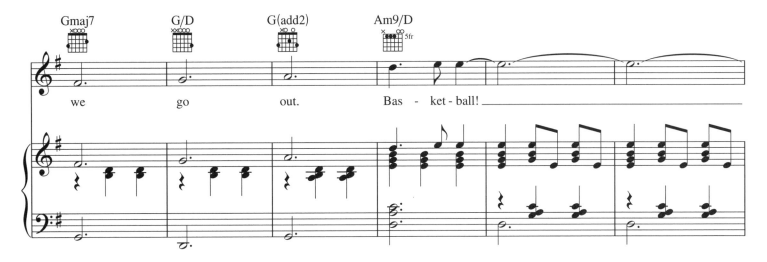

Who ev - er would have dreamed, ev - er would have thought that my

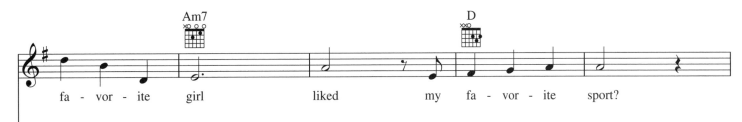

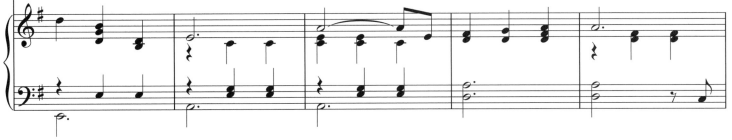

fa - vor - ite girl liked my fa - vor - ite sport?

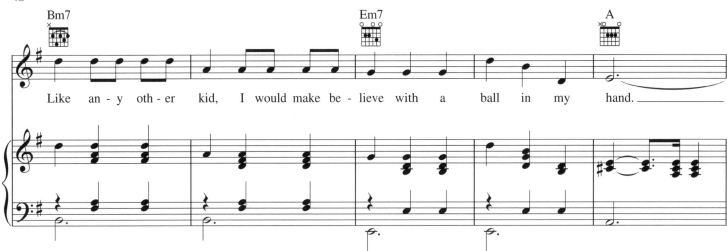

Like an-y oth-er kid, I would make be - lieve with a ball in my hand. _____

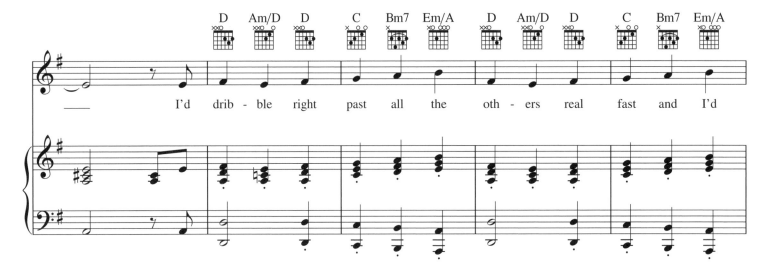

_____ I'd drib - ble right past all the oth - ers real fast and I'd

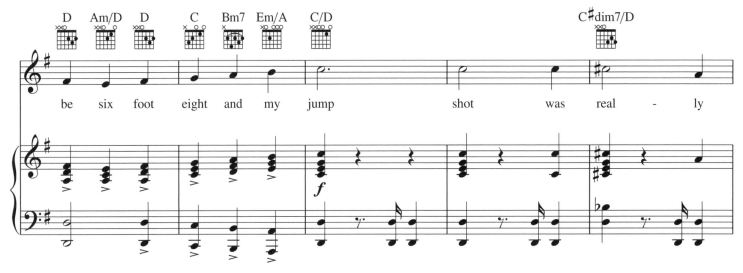

be six foot eight and my jump shot was real - ly

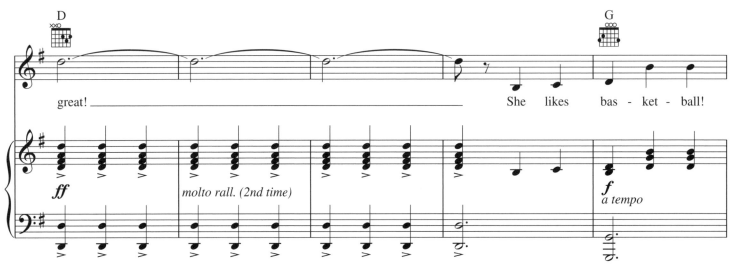

great! _____ She likes bas - ket - ball!

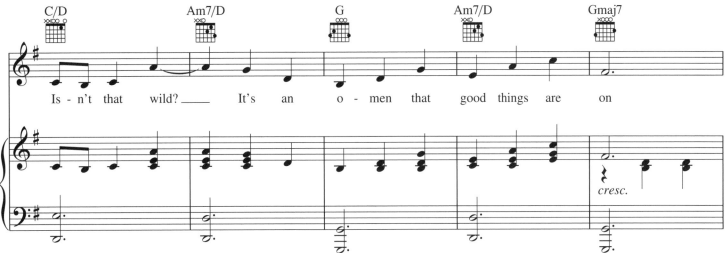

Is - n't that wild? _____ It's an o - men that good things are on

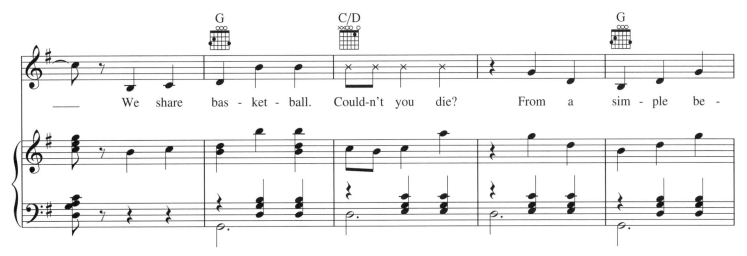

their way— things to share. _____

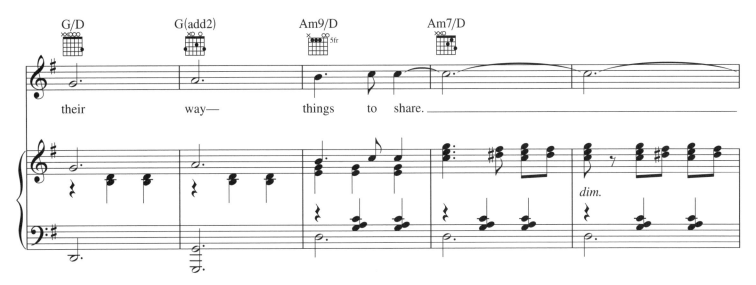

_____ We share bas - ket - ball. Could-n't you die? From a sim - ple be -

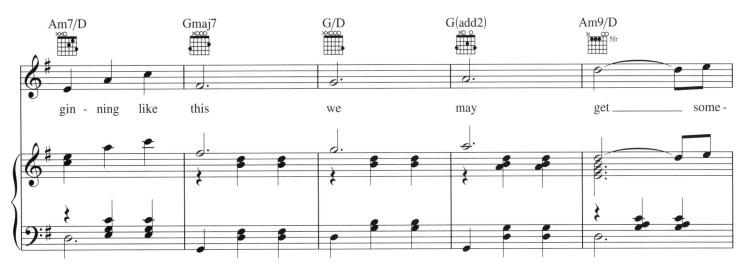

gin - ning like this we may get _____ some -

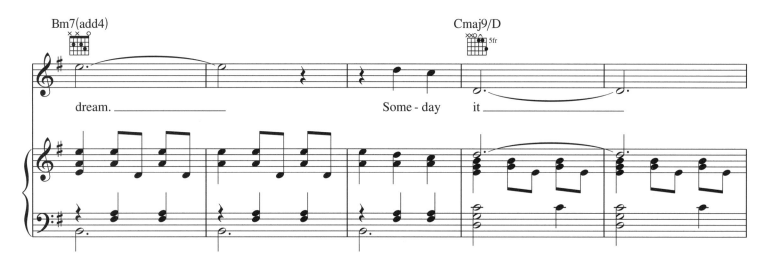

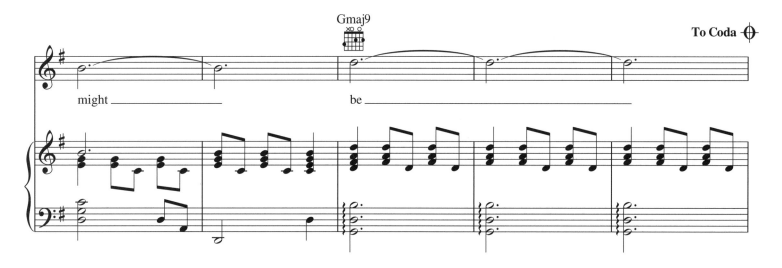

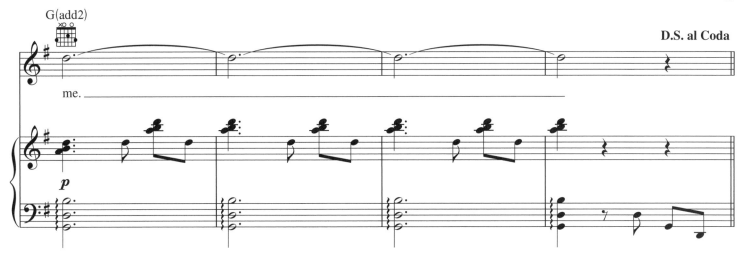

D.S. al Coda

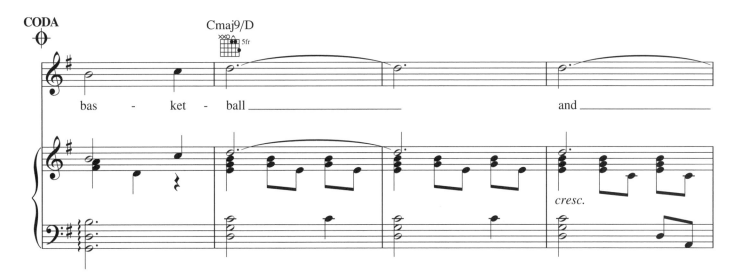

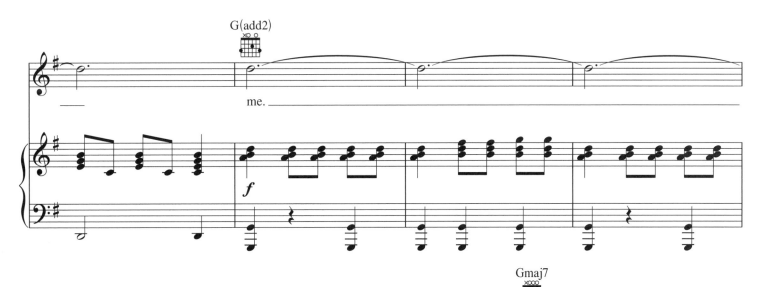

WANTING THINGS

Lyric by HAL DAVID
Music by BURT BACHARACH

SHELDRAKE:

Tell me how long must I keep
When will I learn to re - sist

want - ing things, need - ing
want - ing things, touch - ing

things, when I have so much?
things that say, "Do, do not touch"?

keep want - ing things, _____ need-ing things

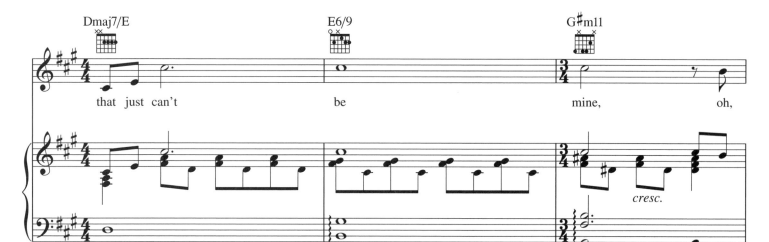

that just can't be mine, oh,

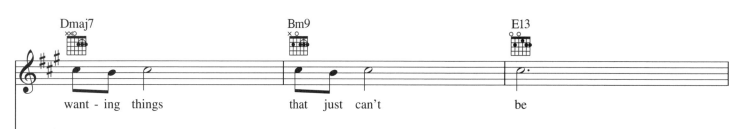

want - ing things that just can't be

mine? _____

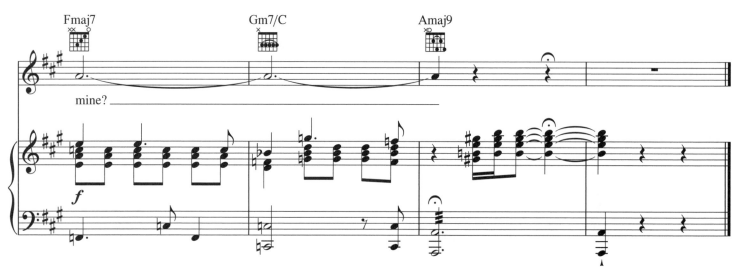

WHOEVER YOU ARE, I LOVE YOU
(Sometimes Your Eyes Look Blue to Me)

Lyric by HAL DAVID
Music by BURT BACHARACH

who - ev - er you are, _____ I love you.

love you.

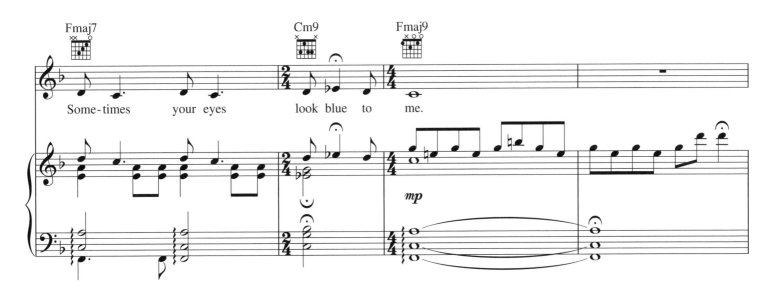

Some - times   your eyes   look blue to   me.

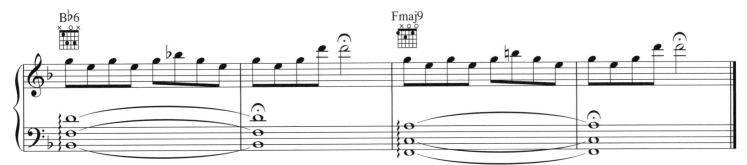

YOU'LL THINK OF SOMEONE

Lyric by HAL DAVID
Music by BURT BACHARACH

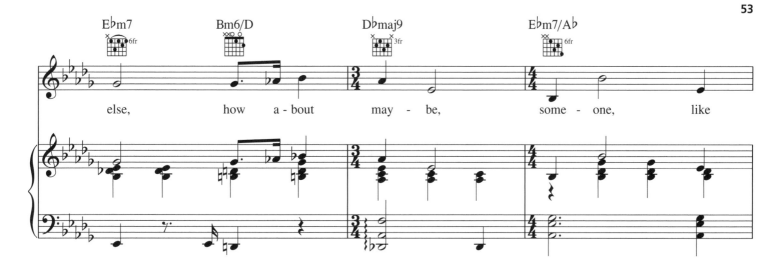

else, how a-bout may-be, some-one, like

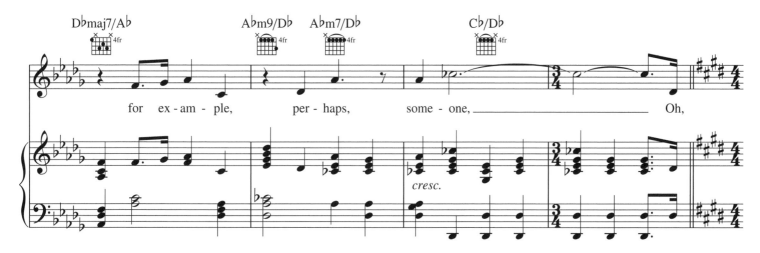

for ex-am-ple, per-haps, some-one, _____ Oh,

BOTH:

you'll think of some-one. who likes you and the things you

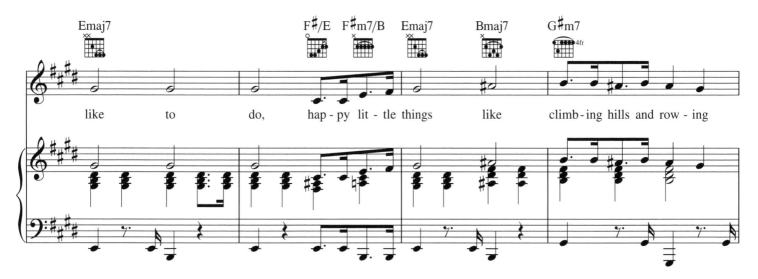

like to do, hap-py lit-tle things like climb-ing hills and row-ing

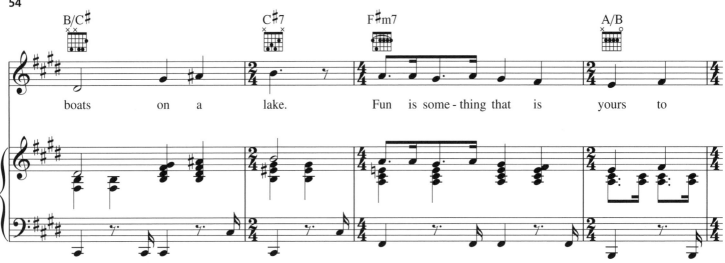

boats on a lake. Fun is some-thing that is yours to

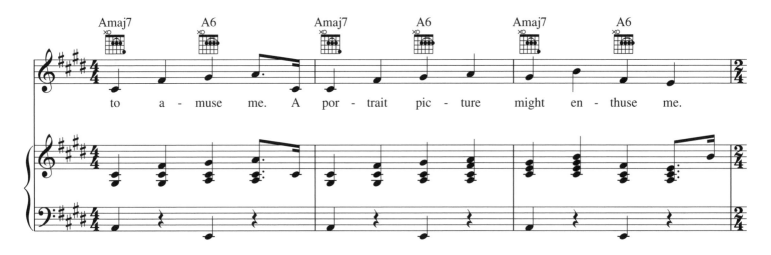

take.   FRAN: I could take up paint-ing _____

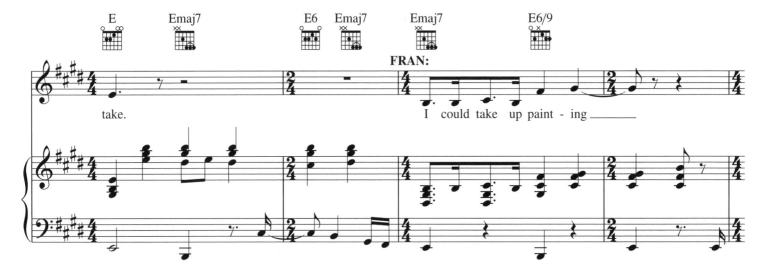

to a-muse me. A por-trait pic-ture might en-thuse me.

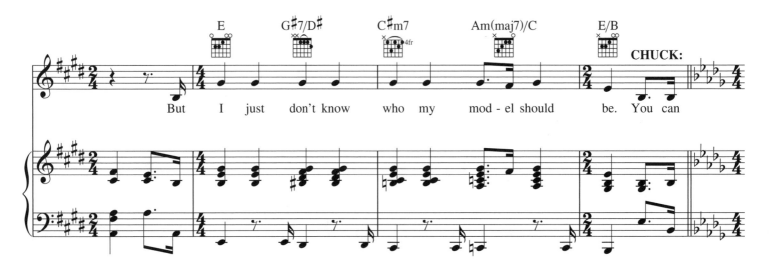

But I just don't know who my mod-el should be.   CHUCK: You can